UDAIPUR
The Fabled City of Romance

Udaipur

Text: ARCHANA SHANKAR
Photographs: PANKAJ RAKESH

Lustre Press
·
Roli Books

Preceding pages 4-5: During the festival of Gangaur, two weeks after Holi, women take images of the goddess Gauri (Parvati) in boats decorated with flowers for a ceremonial bath to the nearest lake.

Pages 6-7: Jag Niwas, the eighteenth-century marble retreat of the maharanas of Udaipur, is now converted to the Lake Palace hotel. On the lakeside is the City Palace, built from 1567 onwards by as many as twenty-two maharanas who inherited it.

Pages 8-9: Maharana Arvind Singh Mewar's son with family retainers, outside Shiv Niwas palace.

Pages 10-11: Kumbhalgarh lies on the topmost ridge of a mountain at a height of 1,087 metres, and is surrounded by thirteen lower peaks.

Following pages 14-15: Birthday celebrations of Maharana Mahendra Singh Mewar.
Pages 16-17: *An overview of Udaipur. The Lake Palace stands centrestage; on the lakeside is the City Palace and Shiv Niwas and unfolding beyond is the white-washed city of Udaipur.*
Pages 18-19: *Palace attendants tying cummerbunds in preparation for a ceremonial occasion.*

Free enterprise in Udaipur.

13

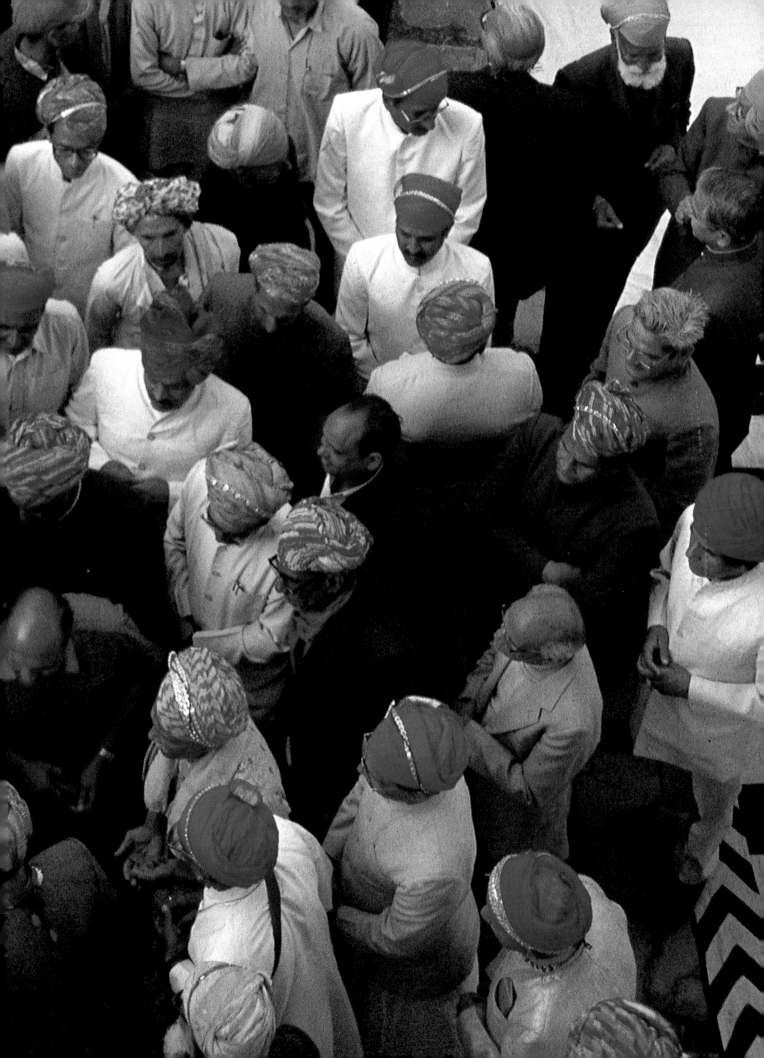

Set in the lush Girwa Valley, surrounded by the Aravallis and interspersed with translucent lakes, Udaipur (meaning 'city of sunrise') is more favoured by nature than most of its desert neighbours. It is situated in southern Rajasthan, 374 kilometres from Jaipur, and is a land of lakeside pleasure palaces, rambling hilltop fortresses, luxuriant gardens with fountains and streams, where bards sing of beautiful princesses and epic warriors. Its annals abound with tales of romance, heroism, chivalry and great traditions.

Udaipur, Chittor and Bhilwara formed Mewar, the largest erstwhile princely state in Rajasthan and a geographically secluded territory whose distinctive physical features played an important part in shaping its history.

Maharana Udai Singh II (1536-1572) laid the foundation of Udaipur as the capital of Mewar in 1567, after the final sack of Chittor by the Moghuls. He built Udaipur (named after himself) between the fortresses of Chittor and Kumbhalgarh. Nestling in an enchanting valley with abundant water and formidable natural defenses, Udaipur was a counterpoint to stark Chittor, 111 kilometres away.

Once, when he was out on a rabbit shoot on a hill overlooking Lake Pichola, Udai Singh met an ascetic who advised him to build his capital on the very spot where they stood. Udai Singh constructed a small temple, Dhuni Mata, at the point where the meeting had occurred. Around it he built a fortress in granite and marble. The ruins of his castle, Moti Mahal, can still be seen on the slopes of Moti Magri (Pearl Hill), the site of the fortress. This was later abandoned when the ruling family moved southwards to the eastern bank of Pichola and began constructing, in 1567, the fortress now known as the City Palace.

Facing page: Built on an island on Lake Pichola, the Lake Palace (Jag Niwas) has a fairy-tale setting. Sprawling over four acres of land, it was the summer residence of the maharanas of Udaipur until 1955.

Udai Singh brought with him the traditions of the Sisodias of Mewar who were considered the 'first' among Rajput royals. The Sisodia dynasty of Mewar is the world's oldest surviving dynasty, spanning seventy-six generations and some 1,500 years. It has outlived eight centuries of foreign domination and its rulers have played a glorious role in medieval Indian history as tireless defenders of Hindu traditions and the kingdom of Mewar. Legend has it that they descended from the Sun God through Lav, the elder son of Rama (seventh incarnation of Vishnu), the hero of the epic *Ramayana*. Even today thirty-six Rajput clans trace their family trees to this mythological root.

Western historians, however, claim that the Rajputs probably descended from Central Asian tribes who, early in the Christian era, came across the northwest frontier via Kashmir. By the second century AD they had moved south to what is now known as Gujarat, founding, as they went, several coastal cities, among which was Vallabhi.

In the sixth century, Vallabhi was sacked by savage invaders from the west. Pushpavati, the queen of Vallabhi, who was pregnant and away on a pilgrimage at the time, escaped. When she heard of the destruction of Vallabhi and the death of her husband, she detoured to the Aravalli hills where, in the course of time, her son Guhil (meaning 'cave born') was born. Entrusting Guhil to the care of the tribal **Bhils**, she committed *sati*. Guhil grew up amongst the Bhils. In the year AD 568, when he was eleven, the Bhil chieftain granted Guhil his first territory. The state of Mewar was thus born; Guhil's descendants ruled over the area for the next seven generations.

The Bhils (their name is derived from *bil*, meaning bow) are the oldest inhabitants of the western and southwestern ranges of Mewar where they have lived since 2,000 BC. The chiefs of Mewar depended to a large extent on the Bhils' numbers, valour and skill in guerrilla warfare in the jagged country;

their active support deterred waves of Maratha and Muslim invaders through the centuries. A golden sunburst, representing solar antecedents, with a Rajput on one side and a Bhil on the other, is still the symbol of the Maharana of Mewar.

LANDMARKS

Udaipur is built around four man-made lakes: Pichola, Fateh Sagar, Rang Sagar and Swaroop

(Garden of the Maids of Honour) to get submerged and so, in 1889, Maharana Fateh Singh built an embankment on it.

Udaipur is a traditionally planned walled city. Its seventeenth-century ramparts were strengthened by huge bastions pierced with eleven gates, each of which was studded with iron spikes as protection against enemy war elephants. Of these only five remain: the **Hathi Pol** (Elephant Gate) to the north; **Kishan Gate** to the south; **Delhi Gate** to the

The City Palace sits on the banks of Lake Pichola and is now mostly a government-run museum.

Sagar. The earliest of these is Pichola, constructed in the fifteenth century by a grain-carrier who dammed the dyke and causeway which he had built to enable his caravan to cross the Ahar river. A century later, Rana Udai Singh built a masonry dam known as Badi Pol, enlarged the lake and named it after the village Pichola, on its shore. In 1678, Maharana Jai Singh excavated another lake, north of Pichola. This lake, however, caused the **Sahelion ki Bari**

northeast; **Chand Pol** (Moon Gate) to the west and **Suraj Pol** (Sun Gate) to the east.

Extending a considerable distance along the east bank of the Lake Pichola, dominating Udaipur, is the majestic City Palace. First built in the year 1567 by Udai Singh, it continued to be rebuilt and expanded upon by as many as twenty-two of the maharanas who inherited it. Built in granite and marble, the City Palace is really four major and several minor palaces forming a single facade. Although it is a blend of Rajput and Moghul styles, its architectural unity has been impeccably maintained.

The entrance to the City Palace is via Hathi Pol, built in 1600, at the northern end of the main street and through the exquisitely carved, triple-arched **Tripolia Gate** which was built in 1725. Between Hathi Pol and Tripolia Gate are eight carved *toranas* or arches. It was once a custom for the maharanas to be weighed on their birthdays under these

dynasty: Sri Charbhujaji, Sri Eklingji, Sri Nathji and Amba Mata. The Rai Angan leads to rooms in which the personal arms and armour, paintings and other memorabilia, depicting the life and times of Rana Pratap, are on display.

Entering the palace, one comes upon a series of courtyards, rooms, corridors and terraces, connected by narrow passages and convoluted stairways in which it is easy to lose one's bearings. The main part of the

The City Palace, viewed from the lakeside.

arches, in gold and silver pieces which were later distributed as largesse to the people. Beyond Tripolia, the Ganesh Deori leads to the **Rai Angan** (Royal Courtyard), built in 1571. It encloses the shrine to the goddess Dhuni Mata. The shrine of Dhuni Mata is the oldest part of the City Palace as well as of Udaipur. It was built on the spot where Udai Singh met the ascetic who suggested the site for Udaipur. The Dhuni Mata temple houses illustrations of the deities of the Mewar

palace is now preserved as a museum. The central area of the City Palace is the seventeenth-century **Mor Chowk** (Peacock Courtyard), built by Maharana Karan Singh (1629-1628) as a new durbar area. Inlaid glass mosaics of peacocks, depicting the seasons, festoon its walls. The peacocks, to which Mor Chowk owes its name, were added more than 200 years later, during the late-nineteenth century, by Maharana Sajjan Singh (1874-1884). Above Mor Chowk is the nineteenth-century

Facing page top: Detail from Mor Chowk, the central area of the City Palace.
Bottom: A refurnished apartment in Udaipur.

This page top: The inlaid glass peacock mosaics in Mor Chowk, from which it got its name, were added more than 200 years after it was first built during the seventeenth century.
Left: The insignia of the Sisodias of Mewar, the acknowledged head of the thirty-six Rajput clans. The Sisodias trace their lineage to the Sun.

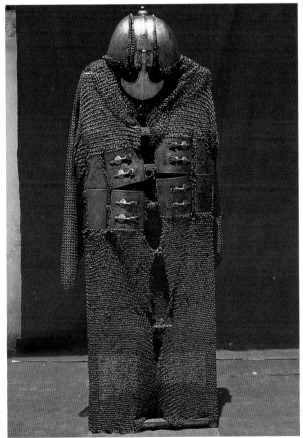

Facing page top: A portrait of Maharana Bhopal Singh, one of the most liberal rulers of Mewar.
Bottom: The City Palace Museum displays the turban in its original folds of Prince Khurram, the rebellious son of Emperor Shahjahan. The prince had sought refuge with the Maharana of Udaipur who hosted him at Jag Mandir for several months. When Prince Khurram was proclaimed Emperor Shahjahan, he was still lodged at Jag Mandir. As a token of his gratitude and respect, the Emperor and the Maharana exchanged turbans, each placing his own on the other's head.

This page top: Inside the Lake Palace. A profusion of mirrors in this room diffuses the sunlight.
Left: The armour, weapons and other memorabilia from the life and times of Rana Pratap are on display at the museum of Rana Pratap in the City Palace.

Surya Prakash with inlaid glass work on its outer walls.

From here one can weave one's way through a host of exotic palaces. **Krishna Vilas**, a memorial shrine, is dedicated to Krishna Kumari, Maharana Bhim Singh's sixteen-year-old daughter who chose suicide over marriage to a rival prince. It contains some of the best miniature paintings of Mewar. **Zenana Mahal** (Palace of the Queens) has its upper windows covered with

City Palace and is entered through the Zenana Dyodhi.

The **Manak Mahal** (Ruby Palace) displays a collection of porcelain and glass. The **Chini Chitrashali**, built in 1717, also houses exquisite Chinese porcelain and glass. The **Choti Chitrashali** is known for its brilliant blue mosaics, while **Moti Mahal** (Palace of Pearls) is embellished with thousands of mirrors.

To the west of the Tripolia lies **Khush Mahal** (Palace of Happiness), built by

The Lake Palace was built in the eighteenth century by the young prince, Jagat Singh, in a fit of pique, it is said, when his father declined him permission to visit the island retreat with a group of friends, and told him to build his own pleasure palace.

latticed screens which served to shield the royal women as they watched the activity in the streets below. It lies to the south of the

Facing page: The inner courtyard of Shiv Niwas palace has a swimming pool and garden, first planted by the maharanas.
Following pages 30-31: Women in conference at Gangaur ghat on the shores of Lake Pichola.

Maharana Sajjan Singh in 1874. To its south lies **Shambhu Niwas**, built in the mid-nineteenth century. **Shiv Niwas**, built later by Maharana Fateh Singh and now a plush guest house, comprises carved pillars, screened balconies and ponds. Its walls are covered with beautiful miniature paintings and frescoes. **Rang Bhavan** occupies the ground floor of the Zenana Mahal. On display here is

an array of gold and silver jewellery and heirlooms.

Rang Bhavan opens into **Laxmi Chowk** (Courtyard of Goddess Laxmi) which houses some of the finest specimens of Mewar miniature paintings. At the far end of Laxmi Chowk is **Osara** (Courtyard of Ceremonies), displaying royal palanquins, *howdahs*, trophies, trumpets and drums.

Within the City Palace is **Amar Mahal**, also known as Badi Mahal or Garden Palace.

The City Palace is open to visitors from 9.30 am to 4.30 pm. The latest addition to the City Palace is **Fateh Prakash** which is next to the Zenana Mahal; this is the current residence of the Maharana and is not open to visitors.

About 400 metres north of the City Palace is the **Jagdish Temple**, the largest temple in Udaipur, built during the last years of the reign of Jagat Singh (1628-1652). The temple is dedicated to Lord Vishnu, the Hindu

On the southern island of Lake Pichola is Jag Mandir, famous for having provided refuge to Prince Khurram before he became Emperor Shahjahan.

It was built between 1699 and 1711 on a twenty-seven metre high natural rock formation, and the ground floor rooms, which stand around the edges of the rock, seem as if they are elevated. They offer an unparalleled view of the surrounding city. A breathtakingly beautiful garden, with flowering trees, ponds, fountains, latticed windows and arched pavilions, is laid out in the centre and is the ideal spot to lull your senses.

Preserver, whose black stone image is enshrined within. It also houses a large bronze image of Garuda, Lord Vishnu's half-man, half-eagle mount. The building has a fine porch and inside several panels depict people playing musical instruments, singing and dancing. Nearby is a smaller temple dedicated to Radha and Krishna.

There are two islands on Lake Pichola: Jag Niwas and Jag Mandir, both one-hour boat rides from the City Palace jetty, known as Bansi Ghat. **Jag Niwas** or the **Lake Palace,** rambling over four acres, is to the north. This dazzling white marble retreat was the former summer palace of the maharanas. Built in 1754, it is now a luxurious hotel. Interspersed with fountains, trees, pools and gardens, it is considered one of the most romantic resorts in the world.

On the southern island of Lake Pichola is **Jag Mandir**, built in the year 1551. It was

and cupolas is the Gul Mahal (domed pavilion). Dotted with palm trees, flowering jasmine bushes, bougainvillaea, roses, nasturtiums and larkspur, it is Jag Mandir's most striking landmark, attracting hundreds of warbling pigeons, screeching parrots and peacocks. The Mohan Mandir stands on a smaller island to the northeastern corner of the lake.

Near the Jag Mandir, on a small raised platform, is the **Natani ka Chabutra**, raised

The Lake Palace hotel. In the distance is the white-washed town of Udaipur.

here that Prince Khurram sought refuge before he became Emperor Shahjahan. Massive sheer stone slabs line the walls of the palace which were once studded with rubies, onyx, jasper, cornelian and jade. Eight stone elephants, facing Jag Niwas, guard the entrance which leads to spacious courtyards with arched pavilions festooned with frescoes and landscaped gardens with cascades and pools. Beneath towering domes

in memory of a *natani* (tightrope walker). It is said that Maharana Jawan Singh (1828-38) once, in a somewhat drunken state, made a wager with a *natani*, promising her half the kingdom of Mewar if she walked the width of the lake on a tightrope, from a village on the west bank of the lake to the City Palace on the east bank. When the *natani* showed every sign of reaching her destination, the rope was surreptitiously severed, thus saving

Legend has it that the young prince Jagat Singh once sought his father Maharana Karan Singh's permission to visit his island retreat, Jag Mandir, with a group of friends. The old maharana declined, telling him to build his own pleasure palace. As a defiant response, the prince did just that. The Jag Niwas, a shimmering fantasy in white marble, moored in the centre of Lake Pichola as if by magic, was built over four acres, and has a fairy-tale quality.

languishing amidst the gentle breezes from the lake.

Jag Niwas was inaugurated on the 1st of February in the year 1746, and the celebrations, which lasted for three days, were recorded by the famed court bard Nandram, in his *Jagat Vilas*. The maharana's grandmother, stepmother,

Inside the Lake Palace.

Jag Niwas, really a complex of palaces, was intended as a retreat for the maharanas of Mewar during the stifling summer months. It was designed to catch the summer breezes as they wafted across spacious granite courtyards, delicately adorned with cusped arches, latticed grills and interspersed with fountains, ornamental gardens, evergreen trees and lotus pools. The erstwhile maharanas spent many evenings in the colonnaded refectories on the water's edge,

his nine maharanis, four aunts, three daughters-in-law and eleven sisters-in-law were present along with hundreds of concubines and maidservants. Lavish gifts of elephants, pedigreed horses, clothes and jewellery were presented to the nobles and court musicians.

Until 1955, Jag Niwas was used as the maharanas' summer residence. Late in 1955, following the decision of the maharajas of Kashmir and Jaipur to convert their respective

PALACE

palaces into hotels, Jag Niwas was also opened to visitors and tourists. Reconstruction work began in 1959 and new rooms were added to Jag Niwas. The old suites, including Sajjan Niwas, which had been the personal suite of Maharana Bhopal Singh, and Sarvaritu Vilas (Palace for All Seasons) and Khush Mahal

Udai Prakash also has a spacious terrace and Kamal Mahal (Lotus Palace) is characterized by inlaid stones in pink and green, set in lotus flower and leaf patterns. Sarvaritu Vilas has intricate inlay work on the arches, carved silver headboards and striking marble patterns on the floor.

The interiors of the Lake Palace abound with wall paintings depicting royal life, crystal and silk furnishings and flawlessly maintained and restored inlay and mirror work. The former

Khush Mahal, formerly the suite for maharanis in Jag Niwas (now the Lake Palace Hotel). Splintered sunlight filters through the stained glass windows in a dazzling play of colour and light. An antique jhoola *(swing) is the focus of this room.*

(Palace of Happiness), which were the former maharanis' suites, were kept as they were. Sajjan Niwas, which contains exquisite Mewar miniature paintings, has an ample terrace from where there is a panoramic view of the city. Khush Mahal has windows made of thick stained glass which filter the sun and throw dappled light across the marble floors. In the heart of this room is an antique *jhoola* (swing).

banquet rooms are now used as reception suites and bars.

Since the Lake Palace opened its doors to its first visitors, innumerable guests have sampled its magic. One of the most romantic hotels in the world, it is redolent of the elegance and graciousness of royal life. Little else bears comparison to this extravagant retreat.

35

the kingdom of Mewar but plunging the girl to her death. Before she died, the girl is said to have cursed the maharana's family, saying that henceforth he would not have any direct heirs. In fact, out of the seven maharanas succeeding Jawan Singh, six had to be adopted. **Arsi Vilas**, another small island near Jag Mandir, is a sanctuary for a variety of birds, including tufted ducks, coots, terns, egrets, cormorants and even kingfishers.

Udaipur also has a large number of *chhatris* (literally umbrellas) or cenotaphs built for its former rulers. The usual style was to have raised platforms with domed canopies supported by columns, ranging from simple four-columned ones to more elaborate structures. Udaipur's earliest *chhatri*, which dates back to 1621, was built in memory of Maharana Amar Singh I (Rana Pratap's son), who was Mewar's first ruler to die in Udaipur. It has a four-faced statue in the centre and friezes at the base, depicting his numerous ranis who committed sati. The cenotaph of Sangram Singh II who, in 1734, was cremated with twenty-one wives, is another fine specimen. It has a fifty-six pillared portico with an octagonal dome in the centre, supported by eight dwarfed pillars.

The old city, which sits on the east bank of Lake Pichola, was built on the undulating ground within the fortifications. The narrow meandering streets here abound in colourful stalls and kiosks, interspersed with old dwellings, temples and gardens, all of which are mirrored in the placid waters of the lake—a picture of composure.

Top: *Detail from a panel from Jagat temple, fifty-six kilometres from Udaipur. Built in AD 960, it is dedicated to the goddess Ambika Mata, a Mother Goddess associated with the Jain Tirthankara, Neminath.*
Middle: *The twin Vaishnava, eleventh-century Sas-Bahu temples at Nagda, north of Eklingji. The larger temple, Sas, is more profusely decorated than the smaller Bahu.*
Bottom: *Outside the Jagdish Temple, built in 1651.*

UDAIPUR'S BYLANES

Outside its city walls, Udaipur is a flourishing provincial city. With the modern town making a transition, old social structures are fraying and growing numbers are moving out of the walled precincts to the densely populated commercial centres. But inside the city, Udaipur is a traditional Rajput town, its rich cultural heritage well-embedded in the land and its people.

Under the ramparts, to the east, is **Bapu Bazaar**, and close behind the City Palace, running from Delhi Pol to Jagdish Temple, is **Bara Bazaar**. In the bustling bylanes of these bazaars you can watch artisans at work, practicing ancient arts and crafts handed down over generations. *Khari* printers emboss floral patterns in gold and silver on plain or printed fabric and block-printers print various patterns and colours on borders, in circles or all over the fabric with hand-held wooden blocks. You can also watch craftsmen carve furniture, puppets and traditional wooden toys. Lacquer work, known as *meenakari*, is another well-honed skill. Brass, silver, copper, jewellery, even pottery, are engraved and embossed in glowing colours.

Udaipur specialises in *lahariya bandhani*, a tie-and-die method which patterns diagonal waves of colour. It is also a centre for *pichhwais* (paintings on cloth, traditionally hung behind images of Lord Krishna). This art form now finds expression on saris, towels, quilts and tablecloths. Stone carving, particularly marble and sandstone, is also highly developed, spurred by the paucity of timber and abundance of sandstone; stonemasons wield hammers and chisels to work up the finest filigree work.

Top: *Ceremonial procession. Within the city, walls are decorated with Mewari folk art.*
Middle: *Outside Jagdish Temple, dedicated to Jagannath, an aspect of Lord Vishnu. Stone elephants flank the entrance.*
Bottom: *Sahelion ki Bari, originally constructed in the eighteenth century by Maharana Sangram Singh, is a small ornamental pleasure garden with lotus pools, fountains and kiosks.*

Colour is complementary to Rajasthani life and in Udaipur resplendent *ghagharas* (Rajasthani skirts, sometimes ten metres around), *cholis* (blouses) and *odhanis* (long veils) are much in evidence. The men generally wear turbans, their colours and patterns varying with the community. Music and dance are also an intrinsic part of their lives. Wandering minstrels, bands of musicians and dancers and dance-drama troupes roaming the city perform in open fields and impart

Bharuji Temple near Dudh Talai, in southern Udaipur.

religious messages, relate local legends, or tell tales of seduction, of unsympathetic mothers-in-law or unscrupulous landlords.

UDAIPUR'S PRECINCTS

There are numerous historic sites and monuments around Udaipur which are worth a visit too. North of the city is the Sahelion ki Bari, a garden retreat created in the early eighteenth century by Maharana Sangram Singh I, as a summer palace for the ladies of his Maharani's *zenana*. The waters of the Fateh Sagar run into lotus pools and fountains which play amidst marble elephants in the *Sahelion ki Bari*. It is a fine example of Hindu landscape gardening and is now a favourite picnic spot.

Five kilometres west of the city and at 750 metres above sea level on a hill called Bansdara overlooking Lake Pichola, is **Sajjangarh**. This palace was built in the late eighteenth century by Maharana Sajjan Singh as an observatory for watching the progress of the monsoon clouds over the surrounding areas; it is also known as the **Monsoon Palace**. From its vantage position the view of the Aravalli hills, lakes, forests and rivers beyond the glimmering white-washed town is breathtaking. During the monsoons, its silhouette is shrouded in a haze of clouds and rain. It is said that Sajjan Singh had planned a nine-storey observatory here, but his plans were cut short by his early death at the age of twenty-six.

Shikarbadi or the Khasi Odi Hunting Lodge, built by Sajjan Singh between 1874 and 1884 as a shooting-box, lies to the left of the Monsoon Palace. The lake palaces and Khasi Odi can be visited by boat.

Three kilometres east of Udaipur is **Ahar,** the ancient capital of Mewar. It has a small museum and *chhatris* commemorating its former rulers. After Chittor was sacked for the last time, Ahar was chosen as the site for Mahasati, the cremation of the maharanas, their kinsmen and nobles. Nineteen *chhatris* commemorate the nineteen rulers who were cremated in Ahar, the most recent being Maharana Swarup Singh's, built in 1861. The pavilions were carved with decorations that resemble the fifteenth-century temples located nearby. In Ahar, beautiful sculptures, images and carved screens have been used in several modern constructions of houses, temples and wells as well.

Twenty-two kilometres northeast of Udaipur, in a remote mountain pass *en route* to Nathdwara is the **Sri Eklingji Temple**. Bappa Rawal, the founder of the Sisodia clan in Mewar, is said to have received religious education from a sage Harita Rishi here. The original temple was built here by Bappa Rawal, but it has since been rebuilt and refurbished by successive maharanas. The Udaipur maharanas regard themselves as *Dewanji* (ministers of) Eklingji, a manifestation of Lord Shiva. The deity is regarded as the real ruler of the state and any power that the maharana possesses is by virtue of his being representative of Eklingji. Sri Eklingji, as the complex of 108 Shiva temples is known, is built on the shore of a lake and is enclosed by a wall. The main temple, made out of white marble, has a huge ornate *mandapa* (pillared pavilion). In the inner sanctuary is a black four-faced image of Eklingji, facing which is a small silver Nandi (Lord Shiva's bull). A statue of Bappa Rawal, standing with clasped hands, faces the image of Nandi.

Two kilometres north of Eklingji is **Nagda** which has several Jain temples, including the eleventh century twin-Vaishnava **Sas-Bahu** (mother-in-law and daughter-in-law) temples. The larger temple, Sas, is surrounded by ten subsidiary shrines and is more profusely decorated than the smaller Bahu which has four shrines. Another Jain temple, **Adbhutji** (meaning peculiar), was built during the reign of Kumbha and is named after a somewhat odd, nine-foot-high image of the Jain saint Shanti Nath which is enshrined inside. Both these temples were built on the edge of the lake, fringed with hills. Submerged within the lake are several later structures.

Nathdwara, situated on the right bank of the river Banas, forty-eight kilometres north of Udaipur, is one of the principal places of pilgrimage in Rajasthan. It is the site of one of the most famous shrines of the Pushtimarga sect of the Vaishava cult, devoted to the child Krishna. The shrine houses a boy-sized image of Krishna, known as Sri

Nathji, said to date back to the eighth century AD. The idol is believed to have been discovered in a rocky hill, Govardhan, and established by Vallabhacharya, a Telugu Brahmin, in a small temple in Mathura in the year 1495. Anticipating a raid by the Moghul emperor Aurangzeb—who proscribed the worship of Krishna—in Mathura, one of the descendants of Vallabhacharya who wanted to find a safe place for the image, removed it from Mathura. Later, in 1671, Maharana Raj

Maharana Arvind Singh Mewar paying homage to Eklingji, the presiding deity of the maharanas of Mewar. Every Monday (the day of Lord Shiva), the Maharana makes the 22 km pilgrimage from Shiv Niwas palace to the temple of Eklingji.

Singh of Mewar offered sanctuary to the idol in Udaipur. However, *en route* to Udaipur, the cart carrying the image got stuck at a place called Sihar; this was interpreted as the divine portent that the image was meant to stay here. In 1691, the famous temple that now houses the black marble statue was built

and the village was renamed Nathdwara, meaning the portal of Lord Krishna. Non-Hindus are not allowed inside the temple. *Pichhwais* (literally, that which hangs behind), the yellow and red cloth scrolls which hang behind the image of Lord Krishna, depict stories from his legendary life. Painted *pichhwais* are a thriving form of folk art and you can see them painted at Nathdwara. Early *pichhwais* have now become scarce and the vegetable and mineral colours which were

work; the first enamel workers were brought into Rajasthan by Raja Man Singh of Amber (Jaipur) from where they scattered all over Rajasthan. A variety of other handicrafts, including gold and silver trinkets, saris, waistcoats, and *meenakari* jewellery, are sold here also.

A few kilometres before Nathdwara is a turning which leads to **Haldighati**, where the historic battle between Rana Pratap and the Moghul forces under Akbar was fought in

A *Shiva* linga *inside Katargarh fort, a smaller fort inside Kumbhalgarh. Katargarh contains 365 temples and shrines.*

once used have been replaced with commercial colours.

Nathdwara is also a centre for *meenakari*

Facing page: *Kumbhalgarh, Rajasthan's most impregnable fortress, fell only once, to the combined forces of the Moghuls, Amber and Marwar.*
Following pages 42-43: *An aerial view of the Ranakpur temple complex. On the banks of Maghai river, surrounded by forests, this secluded pilgrim centre is a celebrated place of worship of the Jains.*

1576. A *chhatri* stands on the spot where Maharana Pratap's valiant horse, Chetak, died after seeing his master out of danger.

Eighty-four kilometres north of Udaipur, deep within the Aravalli hills, off the beaten tourist path is **Kumbhalgarh**. Its inaccessibility through the course of history was reinforced by its forbidding approach through deep ravines, thick scrub and jungles. Kumbhalgarh lies on the topmost ridge of a

mountain, surrounded by thirteen lower peaks. The fort was built at the site of a second century Jain structure after it was won from a Mer ruler, Samprati, who offered himself as a sacrifice to strengthen its premises. Strategically located on a pass bordering the kingdoms of Marwar and Mewar, it is one of the finest examples of protective fortifications. Seven massive gates guard the approach, while seven ramparts, one within the other, were strengthened by rounded bastions and towers which made scaling the walls by ladders virtually impossible. Its serpentine walls, thirty-six kilometres long, were thick enough for eight horses to ride abreast on them. The fort's commanding position atop a hill, 1,087 metres above sea level, also enabled the occupants to see any approaching aggressors from a distance.

To bolster its system of defence, flash lights were mirrored within the first gate, **Arait Pol**. The second gate, **Hulla Pol** (Gate of Disturbance), got its name after the Moghul armies led by Akbar reached this far into the fort after sacking Chittor in 1567. The third gate, **Hanuman Pol**, one-and-a-half kilometres away from Arait Pol, contains a shrine dedicated to the monkey-god, Hanuman. It also houses an image which Rana Kumbha is said to have brought back from Mandore, in Marwar, from where also a beautiful Jhalawar princess was carried away. **Bhairav Pol**, the fourth gate, records an exiled prime minister during the nineteenth century. **Paghra Pol** or Stirrup Gate was erected where the cavalry assembled before battle. **Topkhana Pol** (Cannon Gate) has a secret escape tunnel. The last gate, **Nimbu Pol** (Lemon Gate), has a temple dedicated to Chamunda Devi, a manifestation of the goddess Durga. A shrine of the founding Mer ruler is located nearby. It was in rooms close to Nimbu Pol that the infant Udai Singh was saved by his nursemaid Panna Dai from being murdered by his uncle Bunbir, an illegitimate pretender to the throne.

Several years before the fort was constructed, legend had already glorified **Nar-Chhali**, a small reservoir near the fort. It was believed, that a tiger (*nar*) and goat (*chhali*) drank water together here, a symbol of utopia.

Rana Kumbha never lost a battle and the fort of Kumbhalgarh fell only once to the combined forces of the Moghuls under Akbar, and those of the Rajas of Amber and Marwar (Jodhpur). They succeeded by contaminating the water supply of the fort during the reign of Rana Pratap.

The now derelict ramparts of Kumbhalgarh enclose a smaller fort **Katargarh**. Spread over twelve kilometres, the fortress encloses the decaying palace of Rana Kumbha, barracks of a garrison, 365 temples and shrines—which during their heyday beckoned the devout to *aarti*—dwellings, reservoirs, fields and a village. Also within the confines of Katargarh is the ethereal **Badal Mahal** (Palace of Clouds), 1,000 metres above sea level, built by Fateh Singh during the nineteenth century. From here one has an overview of the rugged Aravallis and the desert of Marwar. On the ridge below the palace of Kumbha is the **Neelkantha Temple**, constructed by Rana Kumbha for his daily worship. The **Navachoki Mamadeva** temple, also constructed by Kumbha, is situated in a gorge below the fort. It houses an image of Kuber (the god of wealth) and contains several black marble slabs, the earliest of which dates back to AD 1491, inscribed with the history of Mewar. There are also two *chhatris*, commemorating Maharana Kumbha and his grandson, the celebrated hero Prithviraj.

To the east of Kumbhalgarh, at Kankroli, lies the **Rajsamand Lake**, built in the year 1660. It has large marble and stone staircases descending from a massive embankment, forty feet high, to the waters' edge which is lined with ornamental arches and pavilions. Princess Charumati, from another branch of the Sisodia family, commissioned these in gratitude to Maharana Raj Singh I, who

Facing page: *The interior of a temple in Ranakpur, ninety-eight kilometres from Udaipur and one of the holiest Jain sites.*

married her to forestall her marriage to Emperor Aurangzeb.

Created by Maharana Jai Singh in 1691, **Jaisamand Lake** lies to the southeast of Udaipur. It consists of seven islands extending over an area of thirty-six square kilometres and is largely inhabited by Bhils. Marble staircases lead into the water, and along the shoreline are several marble *chhatris*. When the lake was inaugurated, Maharana Jai Singh distributed the equivalent of his weight in

small birds, local and migratory, habitate the sanctuary. The four-horned antelope, chinkara, chital, wild boar, sambhar deer, spotted deer, gazelle and panther are also found here. The sanctuary has also enabled the endangered Indian wolf to breed.

One of the holiest Jain sites, **Ranakpur,** is located some twenty-five kilometres southwest of Kumbhalgarh and 100 kilometres from Udaipur. Nestling on a glade on the banks of the river Maghai and sequestered by

The temples at Ranakpur have ceilings carved with fine, lace-like foliate scroll-work and geometric patterns. The domes are made of concentric bands of carving. The brackets connecting the base of the dome with the top are covered with figures of deities.

gold to the people of the adjoining regions. Jai Singh's summer palaces, Hawa Mahal and Ruthi ka Mahal, are set in the foothills overlooking Jaisamand.

The surrounding area which is at its most lush in October, soon after the monsoon, is now a wildlife sanctuary, sprawling over sixty-four square kilometres. Attracted by the expanse of water of Jaisamand lake, a host of

mountains, Ranakpur's beauty is accentuated by its seclusion. Except for temples and a *dharamsala* for pilgrims, it is isolated, in character with the austere ideals of Jainism. The temple complex may be visited from midday to five in the evening.

Facing page: *The images inside Shiva Mandir, Chittor, are among the few which are preserved.*

46

The Adinatha temple, built in the year 1439 and popularly known as **Chaumukha** (four-faced), is at the centre of the temple complex. It is dedicated to the first Tirthankara (Enlightened One), Adinatha Rishabdeva. An inscription in the temple traces its origin to the reign of Rana Kumbha. Legend has it that Dharnasah, a wealthy Jain merchant, had a dream in which he saw the **Nalinigulm Vimana**, the vehicle for celestial beings as described in Jain scriptures. He

sixty-six subsidiary shrines and is the most complex of all the Jain temples. Columned *mandapas*, open porches, projections, niches and panels are superimposed, making for a variety of perspectives. The focus of this elaborate complex is the central towered sanctuary, in the inner sanctum of which is enshrined a four-faced image of Adinatha, each face facing the four directions of the compass. The interior is profusely carved depicting, in panels and concentric circles,

All over Chittor are memorials, reminders of the self-sacrifice of Chittor's defenders.

resolved to create a comparable structure on earth. He took the idea to Rana Kumbha who agreed to requisition a plot of land for the building of a temple, on condition that a township would be built around the temple and that it would bear the royal name; hence the name Rana(k)pur.

The temple was erected at the top of a hill on a raised platform and covered an area of 4,460 square metres. It is surrounded by

narratives from the lives of the Jain saints. It is entered through four doorways.

The **Parsvanatha Temple**, built in the mid-fifteenth century, and the later **Neminatha Temple** which is dedicated to the twenty-second Tirthankara, are two smaller temples facing the Chaumukha. The former enshrines a black image of Parsvanatha in the sanctuary, while on the outside it has erotic carvings, reminiscent of the earlier Khajuraho.

Another temple built around the same time, located nearby, is the star-shaped **Suryanarayana Temple**. It is embellished with friezes of Surya (the Sun god), in his chariot drawn by seven horses.

At the end of Aravallis, on a rocky outcrop, stands the fortress of **Chittor**. Chittor was subject to a long and chequered political history which was inextricably linked with that of Udaipur's. For eight centuries it was the most important bastion of Rajput

(broken) **Pol** where Jaimal of Badnore was killed by Akbar during the third siege of Chittor in 1567, **Hanuman Pol**, **Ganesh Pol**, **Jorla** (joined) **Pol** which is connected to **Laxman Pol** and the main gate, **Ram Pol**, where a memorial stands to Patta of Kelwa who, along with his wife and mother, died fighting to save Chittor.

On a craggy hill, 152 metres high and stretching over five kilometres is the fort. A silence hangs over the deserted palaces and

The palace of Rani Padmini is a replica of the water-pavilion where Alla-ud-din Khilji first caught a glimpse of the legendary queen.

power and its occupation was the primary objective of any would-be ruler. From here, the Rajputs offered a prolonged and determined resistance to Turkish, Afghan, Tartar and Mongol invaders who swept through India in successive waves.

Access to the fort of Chittor is across an old limestone bridge over the Gambheri river. The twisting ascent is met with seven *pols* (gateways): **Padal Pol**, **Bhairon** or **Tuta**

pavilions, temples and towers inside the wall. The present-day town lies at the foot of the hill.

Within the fort stands the oldest palace in Chittor, a ruined palace of Rana Kumbha

Following pages 50-51: *Vijai Sthambha (Tower of Victory), Chittor, was erected to commemorate Maharana Kumbha's victory over Sultan Mahmud Khilji of Malwa in 1440.*

(1433-68). Facing the palace is **Pade ka Mahal**, the Palace of the Heir Apparent. But the fort is dominated by two towers, the **Vijay Sthambha** (Tower of Victory) and the **Kirti Sthamba** (Tower of Fame). The Kirti Sthamba, the older of the two, was built near the eastern ramparts during the twelfth century and was dedicated to Adinatha. It stands twenty-three metres high, is nine metres wide at the base and four metres at the top. A central staircase runs through its seven storeys which are carved with elegant figures of Jain saints. The Vijaya Sthamba commemorates Kumbha's victory over Mahmud Khilji, Sultan of Malwa, in 1437. Built over a ten-year period (1457-1468), this sandstone tower is a masterpiece of Rajput architecture. Rising over thirty-seven metres through nine storeys, it stands on a fourteen-metre square base, and is visible for miles around. Its upper panels which depict Hindu deities are original, but some of the columns have been restored.

Near the Vijay Sthamba is the **Mahasati Chowk** where the ranas were cremated while Chittor was the capital of Mewar. Through the southern gate of the Mahasati Chowk, a flight of steps descends to the **Gaumukh Kund** (Cow's-Mouth Pool) where spring water enters through a stone, carved in the form of a cow's mouth, into the reservoir and then onto a sacred Shivalinga. North of the Vijay Sthambha is the **Mirabai Temple**. Its *mandapa* has a stepped pyramidical roof and parapet surrounding the inner sanctum, which is flanked by four corner shrines.

South of Rana Kumbha's palace, standing side by side, mostly in ruins are the palaces of Jaimal and Patta, two young chieftains of whose bravery ballads are still sung. Nearby are the ruins of the three-storey residence of Chonda who relinquished his claim to

Facing page: Maharana Arvind Singh Mewar and Maharaja Gaj Singh of Jodhpur leading a procession commemorating sati. *Rajputs pray to* Sati Matas, *women who immolated themselves at their husbands' funeral pyres.*

the throne of Mewar in favour of his younger half-brother. Further south, overlooking a large pool, is **Padmini's Palace**, a replica of the water pavilion where Alla-ud-din Khilji first caught a glimpse of the legendary queen. The original palace fell to ruin and the replica was constructed 400 years later.

THE SISODIAS

In the seventh century, Guhil's descendants, called Guhilots or Gehlots, moved north to the plains of Mewar and occupied the territory in and around Nagda, a small town twenty-five kilometres from Udaipur. It was named after Nagaditya, the fourth ruler of Mewar. Subsequently, Ahar, a prehistoric site three kilometres east of Udaipur, became the capital of the Gehlots. Every time Chittor fell to an enemy and before Udaipur was founded, Ahar provided refuge to the ancestors of the present ranas and their kinsmen.

In the seventh century, the Gehlots moved north to the plains of Mewar, changing their name to Sisoda, after a village where they had briefly halted *en route*.

In AD 734, the seventh ruler of the line was accidentally killed by a Bhil tribesman and three-year-old Kalbhoj became king. Kalbhoj, later known as **Bappa Rawal** (*Bappa* meaning father, and *Rawal*, a title of the Kshatriya caste), founded the Sisodia clan in Mewar.

Bappa Rawal grew up as a cowherd in Kailashpuri, a small village set in a narrow mountain gorge, twenty-four kilometres north of Udaipur. He spent much of his time studying the Vedas in the hermitage of the ascetic, Harita Rishi. Here he learned to revere the local deity Eklingji (literally, the single-phallus lord, a reference to Shiva) and eventually Harita Rishi invested him with the title Dewanji Eklingji, a legacy which the succeeding maharanas continued to bear.

Bappa Rawal was fifteen years old when he learnt that he was the nephew of the ousted ruler of Chittor. Giving up his life as a herdsman, he moved to the fortress city of

Chittor and wrested it from Man Singh Mori, the prince of Malwa. However, in the ninth century, the Gehlots were dislodged by the Pratiharas who in turn gave way to the Rashtrakutas and Paramaras. But eventually, late in the eleventh century, the Gehlots recovered Chittor again.

Chittor remained the capital of the Sisodias from the eighth to the sixteenth centuries. The descendants of Bappa Rawal lived here, ruling over an area stretching from Gujarat to

Despite the imposing hill-top fortress, Chittor has endured some of the most famous sieges in history. Its first plundering occurred in 1303, when the Tartar sultan of Delhi, Alla-ud-din Khilji, attacked on the pretext of winning the fabled beauty, **Padmini**, Rani of Chittor and wife of the regent **Rawal Rattan Singh**. After eight months of deadlock, Alla-ud-din offered to lift the siege on the condition that he be allowed to have a glimpse of Padmini. A compromise was

Maharana Mahendra Singh on the occasion of the wedding of his daughter.

Ajmer, until the final sack of Chittor by the Moghul emperor Akbar in 1568. Chitrakuta, the original name of Chittor was derived from Chitrang, the name of a Mori Rajput chief who ruled the area during the seventh century.

Facing page: *Maharana Mahendra Singh of Mewar, his wife and son with his newly-wed daughter and son-in-law.*

reached and the sultan was permitted to see Padmini's reflection on the condition that he came unarmed to the fort.

Accordingly, the sultan went up the hill and glimpsed the reflection of the beautiful Padmini in the lotus pool beneath where she stood. Rattan Singh then escorted Alla-ud-din down to the outer gate where the sultan's men captured the Rana and took him hostage. Alla-ud-din demanded that Padmini be handed over unconditionally as the price for the liberation of the Rana. She acquiesced and a procession of palanquins, ostensibly carrying Padmini and her court of ladies, made their way into Alla-ud-din's camp. Out of the palanquins—several hundred according to some chronicles—a body of Rajput warriors descended. In the ensuing battle, Rattan Singh and several thousand Rajputs were killed. The queen and her cortege, rather than disgrace the Rajput code, performed the ritual *jauhar*

massacre of the populace of Chittor. He then appointed his eldest son Khizer Khan, then only seven or eight years old, as the governor of Chittor and the town was renamed Khizerabad. Rana Rattan Singh's second and favourite son, Ajaisi, who survived the siege, retreated with a small entourage of soldiers to the hills. From here, aided by the Bhils and determined to win back Chittor one day, they carried on a freedom struggle through guerrilla warfare.

Maharana Arvind Singh beside an MG, one of his several cars, many of which have their own historical significance.

Maharana Arvind Singh Mewar at the close of the festivities of Holi.

(the voluntary self-immolation of women). That done, the surviving soldier retinue donned saffron robes, symbolising 'victory or death', smeared their foreheads with the ashes of their wives and sisters and charged through the gates of Chittor to certain death.

Alla-ud-din, incensed by the stubborn fight put up by the Rajputs, ordered a general

In 1326, within two years of Alla-ud-din's death, Hamir Singh (1326-64), grandson of Rana Rattan Singh, liberated Chittor from Turkish rule. During his long reign Mewar

Facing page: *Ceremonial horses being prepared for festivities outside the City Palace.*
Following pages 58-59: *The interior of Rangniwas palace.*

re-emerged as a sovereign kingdom. It was then the only Hindu kingdom left unfettered in northern India; all the other Rajput states had succumbed to the Muslim sultans. To reaffirm their supremacy over other Rajput clans, the Mewar chief was given the title of **Maharana**, (meaning great warrior) as opposed to Maharaja (great ruler) of other Rajput states. Thus Hamir Singh, the forty-third generation of Sisodias to rule Mewar, became Maharana Hamir Singh.

hostility with the Turks. He also excavated silver and zinc mines which became a fresh source of revenue for the state exchequer.

Maharana Lakha was succeeded by his younger son, five-year-old Mokal (1421-1433). Lakha's eldest son and heir, Chonda, had renounced his claim to the throne as a result of some light-hearted banter, but he did enjoy a prominent position in the Council of the state. As the story goes, when Chonda was due to be married, an emissary from Marwar

Ceremonial guards.

For the next two hundred years, the glory of ancient Mewar was revived and sustained. When Maharana Lakha Singh (1382-1421), Hamir Singh's grandson, became king, he had the bequest of a strong kingdom which he strengthened further. He subjugated the frontier chiefs and maintained the traditional

Facing page: *Rajput girls in their traditional finery.*
Following page 62-63: *The Maharana Mewar Research Institute, inside the City Palace.*

came bearing a coconut (a symbol of marriage) from the princess of Marwar, for betrothal to Chonda. Chonda was not present in court on the day in question and his father, then an old man, accepted the coconut and quipped that it wasn't likely that the coconut had come for him. The sally was applauded and repeated, but Chonda took offence at what he considered an unsavoury remark and declined to accept the symbol. The maharana was infuriated at his son's

mystical outpourings in praise of Lord Krishna formed a mass of rapturous songs and devotional poetry which still endure and are universal in their appeal.

Chittor was besieged for the second time in the year 1535, during the reign of Rana Rattan Singh. Sultan Bahadur Shah of Gujarat, lured by Chittor's recently excavated silver mines and supported by Portuguese mercenaries, attacked the fort. It is said that over 32,000 Rajput soldiers were killed and subsequently 13,000 women and children committed *jauhar*. Before she committed *jauhar*, Rani Karnavati (Rattan Singh's widow), sent a *rakhi* (a bracelet symbolizing fraternity) to Emperor Humayun and asked him to rescue Chittor. Flattered that the queen had chosen to enlist his assistance, Humayun intervened, and drove the sultan's forces out of Chittor. He then restored the citadel to Rana Vikramaditya, Rattan Singh's brother, who had escaped the sack. Chittor, however, was in ruins.

Vikramaditya's reign was short-lived. Bunbir assassinated the rana, his nephew, in a bid to usurp the throne and then turned his attentions to Vikramaditya's younger brother and successor, six-year-old Udai Singh. Panna Dai, alarmed by the screams coming from the *zenana*, realised that Bunbir was hunting for her royal charge. She substituted her own son for the sleeping Udai whom she hid in a basket and smuggled out to Bari, the court barber. When Bunbir demanded the whereabouts of the prince, Panna Dai pointed unflinchingly to her sleeping boy, and saw him killed.

Thereafter, Panna Dai wandered from chieftain to chieftain, looking for a refuge for her charge. Eventually, she reached Kumbhalgarh where Udai Singh was brought up as a nephew to the governor Asa Shah until he was fifteen years old, when he was recognised as the true heir and Chittor was restored to him.

Udai Singh II ruled Chittor only briefly. The third and final sack of Chittor in 1567 was by Humayun's son Akbar who had set about to conquer Rajasthan. Udai Singh, in a turnabout from Rajput tradition, fled, leaving Chittor's defense in the hands of Jaimal of Badnore and Patta of Kelwa. For four months the Moghul army was held at bay, but the tide turned when Jaimal was killed by a stray bullet from Akbar's gun. Patta, dressed in saffron, with his mother and young wife by his side, died fighting in the final charge. After a long and bitter struggle which completely devastated Chittor, it was finally abandoned for the lakeside city of Udaipur.

Udai Singh died in 1572, at the age of fifty and **Rana Pratap** (1572-1597), the patriot prince and much-loved hero of Mewar, ascended the throne. Rana Pratap was obsessed with the desire to win back Mewar's old capital and steadfastly refused to accept Moghul suzerainty. (The only other Rajput ruler to do so had been the ruler of Bundi.) In a bid to subdue Rana Pratap, Akbar laid siege and the historic battle of Haldighati was fought in June 1576; it was called so because the battlefield was a *ghati* (a narrow defile) in the mountains where the earth was the colour of *haldi* (turmeric). The Moghul armies were commanded by Raja Man Singh of Amber who, after a matrimonial alliance with Akbar, had chosen to serve him. During the course of the battle Rana Pratap, who disapproved of the implicit subservience of the alliance, hurled a spear at Man Singh. As a result, the imperial army scattered with two Moghul officers in pursuit of Rana Pratap. In the scuffle that followed **Chetak,** the Rana's white steed, was wounded but he carried the injured Rana off the battlefield and died after seeing his master out of danger.

Despite victory for the Moghuls, the battle of Haldighati is significant for the tenacity displayed by the Rajputs, allied with the Bhils, and the art of defensive mountain warfare which Rana Pratap perfected and his successors used.

Rana Pratap and his kinsmen lived in exile following the battle and subsisted on fruit

Facing page: Jagirdars, *titled rural landowners.*

and berries in the ravines for many years. But for the last ten years of his life Rana Pratap ruled in relative peace and eventually freed most of Mewar, including Udaipur and Kumbhalgarh but not Chittor from the Moghuls.

Rana Pratap died in 1597 at the age of fifty-six in Chavand, a village twenty-two kilometres from Udaipur. He remains one of the most celebrated heroes of Mewar; his travails are immortalized in plays, poems,

With peace established, the aesthetic sensibilities of the maharanas of Mewar surfaced and there followed a period of considerable construction. **Maharana Karan Singh** (1620-1628), who succeeded Maharana Amar Singh, vastly improved the palace and its surroundings. He constructed most of the Zenana Mahal (Women's Quarters), Moti Mahal (Pearl Palace), Manak Mahal (Ruby Palace) and Dilkhush Mahal within the confines of the main palace at Udaipur. He

Maharana Arvind Singh Mewar, his wife Princess Vijayraj, their son and daughter at a polo match.

murals and paintings which have become an intrinsic part of Mewar folklore.

The eldest of Pratap's seventeen sons, Amar Singh, succeeded him. **Maharana Amar Singh** (1597-1620) tried to carry out the policies of his father for about twenty years but eventually, pressurized by his nobles, entered into peace treaties with Jahangir. He finally regained Chittor in 1616, on the condition that he would not fortify the city.

fortified Udaipur's city, surmounting its steep walls with domes, arches and turrets, strengthened the dam which encloses Lake Pichola and initiated the construction of Jag Mandir, the island retreat in the centre of Lake Pichola. In 1623, Karan Singh offered refuge to Prince Khurram, the rebellious son of Jahangir, at Jag Mandir which was at the time still incomplete. In 1627, when Emperor Jahangir died and Khurram became Emperor

Shahjahan, he exchanged his turban (which is still preserved in its original folds in the City Palace) with Karan Singh, as a token of gratitude and a symbol of brotherhood. Two centuries later, during the Revolt of 1857, refugee European women and children were also given sanctuary here by Maharana Swarup Singh.

One year after Shahjahan became the Moghul emperor, **Maharana Jagat Singh** (1628-1652) succeeded Karan Singh. He was a

north of Udaipur, Raj Singh built, against the backdrop of the severe seventeenth-century famine, the Rajsamund (Royal Sea) to secure Mewar against another drought. His successor **Rana Jai Singh** (1680-1698), built the Jaisamand Lake, fifty-two kilometres southeast of Udaipur, with a similar dam, surrounded by the summer palaces of the queens of Mewar. Till the building of the Aswan dam in Egypt, Jaisamand Lake remained the largest artificial lake in the world.

A retainer with a family pet, outside Shiv Niwas palace.

A bear entertains tourists.

great architect; he completed Jag Mandir, made several additions to it and gave it his name. He then initiated the building of Jag Niwas, a sprawling pleasure palace. In 1651, Jagat Singh built the Jagdish temple on a hill-top in the vicinity of the City Palace. He also built the smaller Mohan Mandir.

Jagat Singh was succeeded by **Raj Singh** (1652-1680) who inflicted several defeats on Aurangzeb. At Kankroli, fifty-six kilometres

After Jai Singh, several rulers like Amar Singh II, Jagat Singh II, Ari Singh II, Hamir Singh II and Bhim Singh ascended the throne of Mewar. While the Moghuls were kept at bay during this period, the death of Maharaja

Following pages 72-73: *A band playing outside Shiv Niwas palace. Playing the drums in the centre is Maharana Arvind Singh Mewar's son, who is an accomplished drummer.*

Sangram Singh II in 1734 marked the onset of Maratha ascendancy. By the beginning of the nineteenth century, Udaipur was squeezed dry by the Marathas. At the time when Maratha peril was at its worst, Mewar was under a weak and incompetent ruler, **Maharana Bhim Singh** (1778-1828) who is best remembered for the tragic fate of his sixteen-year-old daughter, **Krishna Kumari**. The tragedy involved Jagat Singh, Maharaja of Jaipur, who claimed the hand of Krishna Kumari, and Raja Man Singh of Jodhpur, who disputed the claim on the ground that the girl had been betrothed to his predecessor. Not wanting to offend either ruler because favouring either would have meant war, Bhim Singh prevaricated indefinitely. It was left to Krishna Kumari to resolve the predicament which she did by drinking the opiate extract of the poppy blossom presented to her. Bhim Singh had Krishna Kumari's room frescoed in her memory and called it Krishna Vilas.

In 1818, Mewar, like most of Rajasthan, came under the British yoke.

After the 1857 Revolt and the consolidation of the British empire in India, the kingdom of Mewar—like the other Indian states—was now referred was to as a princely state. The rulers of Mewar retained their pomp and splendour, the ceremony of gun-salutes and durbars but, in the face of rising British paramountcy, were forced to play a secondary role.

Fateh Singh (1884-1930) was the seventy-third maharana of the line. In the tenacious tradition of his ancestors, he steadfastly held out against accepting a subservient status to the British. During his reign, several schools, a college, dispensaries and a railway line, connecting Udaipur and Chittor, were built. He enlarged the Fateh Sagar Lake and completed the elegant Shiv Niwas Palace, to be used as a guest house for his visitors.

Fateh Singh rarely wavered from his convictions. In the year 1903, the Maharana traveled as far as Delhi in two trains, accompanied by 1000 retainers to attend Lord Curzon's Imperial Durbar, but turned straight back to Udaipur without getting off the train when he discovered that he had not been accorded his rightful place in the procession; he had been placed after Hyderabad, Mysore, Kashmir and Baroda. Likewise, he abstained from attending the 1911 durbar.

The British eventually curtailed his powers and though he remained the titular head of Mewar, powers effectively fell upon his son Maharajkumar (heir apparent) Bhopal Singh (1930-1955).

When India became independent in 1947, **Maharana Bhopal Singh** occupied the throne of Mewar. Mewar was one of the first out of about 500 princely states to merge with the Indian Union. Two years later, on 31st. March 1949, twenty-two princely states merged to form the Union of Greater Rajasthan, and the ruler of Udaipur was the acknowledged head.

Maharana Bhopal Singh, although bound to a wheelchair since the age of sixteen, was a remarkably liberal ruler, appreciative of the need for change. He was also a great educator and established dozens of schools and colleges in Mewar.

Several generations ago, Maharana Sangram Singh II (1710-1734) had four sons; the first born, Jagat Singh II succeeded him, and the other three founded the Bagore, Karjali and Shivrati lines. All the subsequent maharanas of Mewar were linear descendants of Sangram Singh II.

Bhopal Singh was the first natural-born son to succeed to the throne after five consecutive adoptions. In 1939, Bhopal Singh adopted seventeen-year-old Bhagwat Singh who was then a schoolboy in Mayo College, Ajmer, from the Shivrati branch of the family.

One year after Maharana Bhagwat Singh (1955-84) ascended the throne, on 1st November 1956, the state of Rajasthan came into being. The Rajput rulers relinquished their sovereignty but enjoyed privy purses which were paid from public funds until 1969, when the Parliament decided to do away with the institution of royalty. In 1971, the rulers of the erstwhile princely states were 'derecognised', their privy purses and titles abolished in one stroke.

One of the earliest decisions Bhagwat Singh took to ensure the survival of his property was to establish a private company to which he sold Jag Niwas, Jag Mandir, Fateh Prakash and other lands on the shores of Lake Pichola. He reworked Jag Niwas to a charitable trust which he called the Maharana Mewar Foundation. The money earned from this trust was to devolve to social welfare and education. This trust runs the

himself from the family and subsequently, when his father Bhagwat Singh died, his will unequivocally disinherited Maharajkumar Mahendra Singh.)

Today, **Maharana Arvind Singh**, who is married to Princess Vijayraj, the grand-daughter of the ruler of Kutch, administers the House of Mewar.

Beginning with Guhil to whom the first territory was bestowed during the sixth century AD, the maharanas' position was

Shebnai players and caparisoned elephants welcome visitors.

City Palace complex. Bhagwat Singh also instituted another trust called the Maharana Mewar Institution Trust of which the Managing Trustee was to be his second son, Maharajkumar Arvind Singh; both Shiv Niwas and Shambhu Niwas are inalienable from Arvind Singh and his heirs.

(In 1983, one year before Bhagwat Singh died, his first-born, Mahendra Singh, had filed a civil suit seeking to partition the family inheritance. By this act he effectively severed

based on what was granted on trust to their ancestors; they were the trustees of Eklingji For seventy-five generations, the maharana was the custodian of the State of Mewar. Now, in the seventy-sixth generation, Maharana Arvind administers the House of Mewar. As the successive Maharanas through history have done, Arvind Singh makes a pilgrimage to the temple of Eklingji every Monday. The emblem of Eklingji leads the procession and the Maharana follows.

75

oyalty traditionally encouraged the art of painting as one of the sixty-four *kalas* (fine arts) of ancient India and almost every princely state of Rajasthan developed a school of its own. The school of miniature painting in Mewar was one of the earliest, distinct from the Bundi school which was its offshoot. The Kishangarh and Jaipur (Amber) schools of miniature painting developed much later.

The Jain miniatures of illustrated manuscripts of the thirteenth to fifteenth centuries paved

manuscript illustrations. The Mewar school was also related to this school in many respects.

Mewar paintings were characterized by the use of simple, strong and luminous colours with a rich effect. The treatment was bold, with human, animal, vegetative and floral forms being depicted in minute detail. The landscape was accentuated so that the figures blended with it.

Jayadeva's twelfth century Gita Govinda *was a pervading subject for Mewar miniatures.*

the way for Mewar miniature paintings. The most frequently illustrated Jain texts were the *Kalpasutra* and *Kalakacharya katha*. The style was linear, with sharp, angular contours, the faces generally in profile but showing both eyes. The colours were few, predominantly black, blue, green and yellow, and a patch of red comprised the background. But before this period, a more decorative style, which culminated in the *Chaurapanchasika* (fifty songs and a thief) series, was used in several

The main subjects were the Sanskrit texts or Braj Bhasha poetry such as *Ragamala* (garden of melodies), *Nayika bhada* (the traditional classification of lovers), and *Krishna lila* (Krishna stories). Lacquer red frequently served as the background. Illustrations from the *Ramayana* and *Mahabharata* were also part of the repertoire.

By the end of the thirteenth century, miniature artists were being lured to Delhi by the early sultans. The blend of Indian and Persian art fructified in the Moghul miniature school of painting.

MINIATURES

For the most part, the Mewar school remained insulated from Persian influence but later paintings, done after Mewar's treaty with the Moghuls, demonstrated a synthesis of the two styles, with the vigorous Rajput *kalam* yielding to the pleasing colours of Moghul miniature paintings.

By the end of the sixteenth century, the Mewar

Court painting flourished, reaching its zenith under Amar Singh II (1698-1770). Under Sangram Singh II (1710-24), painting became more prolific. It recorded pictorially the life of the rulers of Mewar and the customs of its people. The style became more intricate and was executed with the finest brushes, made from the throat-hair of squirrels and sometimes only one hair thick. In several paintings, the high marble walls of the Udaipur palaces, domes, balconies, walls and niches constituted the setting for

Idealised lovers, personifying the Radha-Krishna myth, are a recurring theme in Mewar paintings.

school entered a new phase. During the reign of Jagat Singh I (1628-52), there was a new upsurge in Mewar painting. Jagat Singh's principal artist, Sahibdin, carried forward the tradition of religious manuscript painting, inherited by the Rajputs, and overlaid it with the Moghul style. Further impetus was given by Karan Singh I (1620-28), who erected the Choti Chitrashali inside the Udaipur City Palace and decorated it with religious pictures and portraits which, although essentially Hindu in character, absorbed Moghul influences.

elaborately dressed maharanas and their nobles. The local landscape was now depicted naturally, in contrast to the earlier paintings in which trees, hills, rocks and water were stylized.

The masterpieces of Mewar miniature painting are among the best in the world and virtually every fine art gallery in Udaipur has a pool of artists making modern-day reproductions of the classics, some of which are preserved on the walls of the City Palace, Shiv Niwas and the Lake Palace.

*R*ajasthan's population includes many tribals, like the Bhils, Minas, Sahariyas, Damariyas, Garasias, Gaduliya Lohars and Bhil-Minas. The Bhils and the Minas are the largest group. The tribals, who constitute 12 per cent of the state population, share common traits but their costumes and jewellery set them apart from each other. A turban is the most visible part of a man's dress and most tribals can be identified by their typical, vividly-coloured turbans. The men of the Bishnoi community, however, wear white turbans and their women can be

singled out for their intricate and elaborate nose rings. On the forehead many women wear the borla *or* rakhri, *a silver ornament that defines the hairline. Women all over Rajasthan festoon themselves with heavy silver jewellery and loads of ivory or bone bangles worn from the wrist to the shoulder. The vibrant colours of the headgear and costumes are heightened by the use of the very characteristic tye-and-dye* (bandhini) *method of printing fabric, and are in contrast to an otherwise arid landscape.*

First Published 1997
© **Lustre Press Pvt. Ltd. 1997**
M-75, Greater Kailash-II Market,
New Delhi-110 048, INDIA
Phones: (011) 6442271, 6462782, 6460886
Fax: (011) 6467185

ISBN: 81-7437-072-2

Text Editor: Bela Butalia
Typesetting: Naresh L. Mondal
Production: Naresh Nigam, Abhijit Raha
Concept & Design: Roli CAD Centre

Photo Credits:

Aditya Patankar: pages 22, 49
B.P.S. Walia: pages 34, 37C
Ganesh Saili: pages 20, 27A
J.L. Nou: pages 2 (A, G), 3E, 26A, 30-31,
45, 47, 52, 56A, 58-59, 76B, 79B
Karoki Lewis: pages 78 (B, E, H, I), 79I
Lustre Press Library: pages 3 (A, E), 16-17, 23, 77A
Pramod Kapoor: pages 2 (B, C, E), 3D, 4-5, 29, 37B,
40, 46, 78 (A, C, G), 79 (A, C, D, E, F, G, H)
Rajpal Singh: pages 2D, 25B, 36 (A, B, C),
38, 71B, 75, 76A, 78D
Sanjay Singh Badnor: pages 12-13, 28, 48,
50-51, 56B, 57, 61, 78F

Printed and bound in Singapore